The Maharani's
New Wall
and
Other Poems

Other books by David Ray

X-Rays: A Book of Poems
Dragging the Main and Other Poems
A Hill in Oklahoma
Gathering Firewood: New Poems and Selected
Enough of Flying: Poems Inspired by the Ghazals of Ghalib
The Mulberries of Mingo and Other Stories
The Farm in Calabria
The Tramp's Cup
The Touched Life
Not Far From the River
On Wednesday I Cleaned Out My Wallet
Elysium in the Halls of Hell
Sam's Book

The Maharani's
New Wall
and
Other Poems

David Ray

Wesleyan University Press
Middletown, Connecticut

To Judy

Some of these poems first appeared in: *Amelia, Chandrabhaga* (India), *Chariton Review, Everywhere, From Mt. San Angelo, Hampden-Sydney Poetry Review, Illustrated Weekly of India, The Kansas City Star, The Missouri Review, National Forum, New Letters, New Quest* (India), *Okike* (Nigeria), *Ploughshares, Prairie Schooner, Sotheby's Contest Anthology* (England), *Span* (India), *Stone Drum, 2Plus2* (Switzerland).

The author is grateful for all of the encouragement and assistance that has sustained his work, and especially for awards from the Council for International Exchange of Scholars (an Indo-U.S. Fellowship), the Bellagio Study and Conference Center of the Rockefeller Foundation, the University of Missouri–Kansas City, the Virginia Center for the Creative Arts, the Leighton Artists' Colony at Banff, and Yaddo. The author is also grateful to The Arvon Foundation and *Amelia* magazine for prizes granted to individual poems in this collection.

Library of Congress Cataloging-in-Publication Data

Ray, David, 1932–
The Maharani's new wall and other poems.
(Wesleyan poetry)
I. Title. II. Series.
PS3568.A9M34 1989 811'.54 88-10650
ISBN 0-8195-2164-7
ISBN 0-8195-1165-X (pbk.)

Manufactured in the United States of America

FIRST EDITION
WESLEYAN POETRY

Contents

The Maharani's
New Wall
and
Other Poems

Two Before the Temple

Her brother takes in darkness
while she gives off
the light,
what radiance is found
in cheesecloth cape,
teeth, marbles
of the eyes.
That brother wears
a shroud like Nosferatu's,
full of shadows, midnight.
Even here at noon before
the Pushkar temple
he may sink his fangs
for tourist blood.
He glowers, broods, will not
in good cheer take
my spill of sympathy,
accept grim poverty,
that token rupee.
To hell with you,
he says with lowered eyes
while his sister charms
rupee after rupee,
smiles on cue, rests
a knee that I might later boast
my cubist composition—
all dark wedges artful,
stones of street and wall
all broken for my genius.
Halfway round the world
I wait. She'll dance.

A Chat with a Holy Man

Baba told me,
his hair in curls, long ringlets
a nest for his shining face:
"I'm blissed out all the time."
Baba told me, when I asked
if he could play the flute,
since one was stuck
inside his dhoti, wrapped
round him like a sheet:
"I play my own Being, that's all."
Baba told me, when I asked
how long each day
he meditates: "Meditate,
what's that? I'm just
blissed out by life."
"And that?" I pointed to
his begging bowl, of brass
and walnut wood.
"I do all right," he said.
"Next week I fly
to Kashmir, then Canada.
The States won't let me in.
They want a man to lie
and claim he has a job,
some source of income,
some wife, perhaps, or friend.
But I can't lie, you know."
And he looked me in the eye
and laughed and asked if I
might take a close-up,
Baba on the road of life,
between two fragile mountains.

My Rooftop Room

It's downhill past the sacred cows,
running gutters, early scooters—
three or four riding each, saris
ballooning from sidesaddle girls—
past squatters by their hillside tents
of stitched gunnysacks, propped with tin,
the women tending fires or bent
to pick lice from their children's hair.
On piles of garbage, feathers, dung,
and hair the barber tosses out,
small boys wrestle or fly their kites.
Rickshaws, bikes, and strolling women
head toward the bleak industrial city
that Gandhi disapproved. Smoky views
of Babel line the roadside, obscure
the lilac sky. Great towers stand
laced in bamboo cage, a labyrinth
of scaffold, plank walkways wrapped
round stone. Bright sweeper women fly
from dust, a mushroom cloud behind them.
Their brooms churn up the earth.
They're busy as a fine machine,
six dancing round in swirling gyres
to do a roadside gutter. A pony's tied
where I make my left, bike bouncing
through high yellow arch—it's called
an ogive. Then I'm in where two
peacocks strut beside a fountain.
Monkeys clamber walls and cup
their mouths as if they might screech
something indiscreet. The crazy lady sits
upon her bench and plays with statuettes
of Krishna, Hanuman, and Kali. Behind her
the old man sits with hash pipe. I wave,

am quickly up the side stairs, past turds
of cats and toddlers of the Rajput clan.
Great oaken doors are opened wide
upon my rented roof. I fall into this light,
check with quick peeks through archers' slots
that fields below are quite all right today,
then face my rooftop room, its lazy fan left on.
Ancient amber photos lean, look down.
Best chance for me, I know, is here,
a silent morning adrift toward noon.

Jaipur

A monkey scampers on the wall
that's terra cotta, not the pink
most guidebooks persist in claiming.
And my friend Sohan Singh, who sits
under his front verandah arch,
looks out on terraces and trees
left by his Rajput ancestors,
who built a castle on the hill.
His tiny dogs have names of gods,
bark at peacocks and the mongoose
tied near cobras bagged in burlap.

Now tourists come by flocks and droves
to crane their necks while a guide bobs
a candle toward sparkling skies
where stars in shards of mirror shine—
all this in darkness though midday.
Most bourgeois husbands want to know
where the harem thrived—its rooms form
a maze of walls viewed by standing
on a parapet. Roof's removed,
a beehive viewed in cutaway.
There women in a labyrinth
worked like slaves to please their king.

Only he and his eunuchs knew
just where they kept the *vish kanya*,
the special girl who sipped poison till
her kiss was like the cobra's.
She was the gift for friend betrayed
or enemy deceived, her love
a final, fatal, facile trick.

But all that's past. My friend rents rooms
where Japanese read paperbacks
or watch the lacquered rifles glow,

crossed with black spears upon the wall
near lithographic battle scenes
of tigers fighting elephants.
We crack our peanuts, leave the shells
in Pan Am ashtrays tourists swipe
but then get bored with—thus they're left
on Singh's front porch, with souvenirs
of five-star hotels and London bars.

Two girls navigate the garden
in bright red saris laced with gold.
Their nose rings glint, flash diamond motes.
And the peacocks scatter, leaving
green tribute feathers on the path.
Under the tamarinds the doors
of weekend cottages are flung
wide open. Wrinkled sheets attest
to last night's orgy or collapse
when sad-sack lovers just returned
from moonlit Amber or the Taj
quarreled or bogged down with accounts—
so many rupees in their wake.

The tour group's gone and I'm alone
with two frail servants and Krishna—
Singh's eldest daughter, married but
flighty as a bird, dark as teak—
with eyes that gleam as she pours tea
from the trunk of an elephant.
We gaze out where black cannons face
the drive, their red wheels stilled and blocked.
And one's a true old Gatling gun—
two dozen rifles bundled round
like a deadly sheaf revolving.

Outside these walls those not so fair,
grim princesses of dust, lift pans
of heavy sand upon their heads
or whirl in groups of six to make
a machine of brooms, dancing girls
whose speed through gutters rivals wind,
a human cyclone flinging dust
and redistributing the earth.

Last night that German by the pool
stood beside his friend at sunset,
a woman courted, compromised
in public with him for a week.
I fear he'll leave for Hamburg soon
while she must stay to face disgrace.
Besides, it's clear he can't live long—
he's coughing out his bloody lungs.
And yet he came because he dreams
of a love that's perfect, great pearl—
the Taj Mahal or mosque, one tear
that trembles off earth's riven cheek.

Near me now, a crow takes his chair
and squawks it out with a peacock,
neck of sapphire blue yet yowling
like an alley cat. Beyond them
my clay path leads through fields. Green birds
await me there, will flutter up
behind me like a cape, my bike
with silver wheels awhirl in light.

Hash

When I first saw
that old man
in his red turban,
nearly toothless,
I thought he was
a holy man, a *sannyasi*
for sure, such a wondrous
spirit, his smile
like a child's,
forgiving (as if he had guessed
my sins), candid,
wise. Now I know
him better, and he offers
me hashish, some of his,
and we sit on the verandah
of Sohan Singh's hotel.
And Sohan says, "Go ahead;
this old man loves you,
wants you to have
some of his hash."
But I just sit
smiling and admiring
that enlightened
remarkable holy man
in his red turban,
with his human secret.
Hell, it's not a secret;
he offers it to everyone—
the tourist women
in their new saris,
the collector of used bottles,
castrato singers at the fountain,
shepherd kids who pass with goats,
and all who laugh or cry with him.

A Statue of Gandhiji

From our window
on the second floor
we can look out level
at the statue
of Gandhi,
a silhouette in dusk
raised high
on a marble plinth.
He steps out
with a staff
as into the bustle
of the modern mob,
high above
rickshaws, camels,
strolling cows.
As it grows dark
he looks
like a peacock,
his shawl the folded
feathers he never
unfurled in pride.
Nor would he,
I think, have raised
himself so high.
To honor men
we make them truly
shadows of themselves,
their small,
their fragile selves.

By a Lake Near Jaipur

We sit on cremation ghats over water,
their roofs like stone umbrellas.
Thin grass has grown on the platforms,
ripples in breeze, souls of the long departed.
On this spot the Rajput king became flames,
ash of his body blown out over that glimmering lake
where the white lotus float now as then,
by the myriad. A stone slab propped
against a palm tree shows him in life,
on his horse, and his two wives standing,
their arms crossed just as after
they crawled up, lay beside him
willingly on the great stone platform
for suttee, both of them lying
like sisters together, taking the fire.
Year after year the wind takes them
as ash, as sand, out to the routes of cranes
and white egrets said to be souls of the gods.

The Rooftop Room

I rented it cheap, that terra-cotta room at the top
of the castle still half home, yet half hotel—
full of ancient dusty photos of the Rajput lords
with their turbans and swords—and an overhead fan
idly whipping the air. Then one weekend
the landlord asked for the key, he didn't say why.
But all was clear by midmorning Monday,
for newly-wed lovers do not pick up
after themselves. A strand of her long black hair
lay thick as a mare's upon the pillow.
And the sheets told their story, slashed out
in red ink. It was my task in that midmorning sun
to ignore this distraction. But like a forgetful
peacock I wandered the roof where, it seemed,
they had spent most of their time. A bottle not quite
empty stood by two glasses, lipstick on one.
Against the ocher wall of my room was a bureau
with pitcher, basin, towel laid aside, comb
of genuine tortoise shell left behind, holding one
glossy hair long enough to come to her ankle.
Sun struck the scene, nothing but blue sky in the mirror
where there had been stars. Inside, over a candle,
another mirror was angled—so old and flaked
it had seen a thousand such scenes. I grasped
that the high and ornate charpoy with enameled black
posts rising halfway to the ceiling was kept for just
such occasions—left unrequired for years at a time,
then offered for love on its altar.
There are times when life is so empty you can do nothing
but gaze after, like a homeless pup watching a parade.

The Unauthorized Colonies

The unauthorized millions have multiplied and now,
flooding into the cities, cannot be denied.—V. S. Naipaul

They live in the city
just as if it were country,
the girls reaching up,
stretching, pulling their bodices
high, revealing their brown
kissable bellies as they tug
at the eucalyptus branch,
jumping up for a moment, actually dancing
off the ground, feet dangling till the taut
branch breaks and gives a green leaf to their goat.
And the old shepherd with his crook meanders
along the street as if a vast meadow,
not turbulent traffic, rises up before him.
He ignores loud insolent horns, turbaned
policemen who hammer the air, their angry eyes
chasing him. With his sheep marked with red henna,
oblivious, he pays them no heed, like peasants
in battles. Others sit on the ground
or on their hemp-and-stick charpoys outside tents
in their unauthorized cities of canvas.
And they are beautiful as damsels in towers
save that they have no walls and their floors
are of sand. Yet these women afford
plenty of marigolds to weave in their hair
and I have seen them giving their laughter
                              to the smoky air.

The Maharani's New Wall

The maharani on her hill
with battlements that catch
the orchid sunset in silhouette
has tired of looking out
on peasants dug in as if
scratching for a beachhead.
They came on waves of sand
beneath her eagle's eyrie,
her nest of bullion eggs,
her dungeon holding gold.
She's high above their half-tents,
tied straw and tin that roofs
unwelcome peasantry.
One day she waves an arm
where bangles coil and glitter
and orders a great wall raised
all round her private mountain.
So the dhotied men and women
with bare bellies squat to break
hard granite for her wall.
In midday the sun will not forgive
and seems to have it in for all
who must have sinned
in one past life or other.
They're sentenced now to dust
and a life of ceaseless labor.
I pass them on my bike and see
how they caress knife-sharp rocks
to hew them, and I wonder how
such chunks will ever make a wall,
the smooth lines I see advancing
as the hundreds squat and lift.
A bronze fat supervisor sits
on a chair with a black umbrella

held by a peon near him. Another
waves a fan. No breezes stir
to dry the dripping sweat upon
a sari-wrapped old gramma.
She never stops to wipe but lifts
a heavy pan of mortar on her head
as if it were a weighted crown.
The maharani up above looks down
at times to watch her busy ants,
who cost a rupee, maybe two
each day, each head, for lifting
stone from dawn to dark, pieces
of a puzzle that lock together like
stone lovers of Khajuraho or Konarak,
temples made with just such labor
though they're more ecstatic
when the light strikes sandstone breasts
or a buttock that's caressed. This wall
is damn near perfect, holding sand
and trees by tons in place, but not
this wretched flotsam of the poor
that's taken root for centuries.
They scramble in and out now
and over the boundary twine. But when
the job is done they'll be blocked
from ancestral paths, homes dug out
by hand when nomads vowed to stay.
Like a queen who guards her castle
the maharani strolls above, peeks down.
Dark hawks and vultures
line her castle while down below
her hordes of peasants sweat and hope
to please her, nor do they leave a way
to crawl back home in moonlight.

The system's far too rigid
for such a flaw or gap. In fact,
the wall's as nearly perfect
as a work of man can be at half
past noon in the desert of Rajasthan—
if you like the works of men
yet care not for those men
or their women or mewling brats
who are clutching at the sand
while their eyes are rolling round
to seek their patroness in dust.

The Optometrist

"If this man tells me one more time
about his half a kidney left
or the four stones the doctor found
when they cut him open or shows
his scars again, I swear I'll scream.
We should have brought our own clean cups.
The tea's all right, if boiled enough.
It's the cup's brim you've got to fear
unless you want to die. Why can't
you ever be the one to think
of just such facts? It's always me.
Amazing how they live like this,
my hardly shy optometrist, his ample wife
—I see her breast each time she bends.
I swear they'll never learn that we
will not, *cannot* drink their water.
She offers yet again—and those sickly cakes
one girl ran out to buy, covered with
a hundred flies, an inch of dust. We sit
beneath their calendar, a big-trunked
elephant on it, a god to them. He's said
to bring good luck. But what's he brought
to *this* incense-laden room, its ocher air?
In the States optometrists are stinking rich.
He works six-day weeks for this. 'I like
my work,' he says. 'No picture shows for me! . . .
God's good to me!' I wonder which god he means.
Bars on windows keep bandits out. And now they get
their snapshots down, blow dirt off. Christ,
there's one of when they married! Shy then,
I'd say, and she looks somewhat puzzled.
Knows how it will go, I guess. They show
their kid who died and one of how old granddad
looked the year he passed. And then that aunt
who reached one hundred ten, he swears, back

in Pakistan before they fled in 1947
to shifting sands of Rajasthan. They sit
upon the bed, my optometrist, his wife,
two girls, a family scene, all quite at home.
If asked to sit like that by us, our girls
would snarl like cats. They need their space,
their income from our handouts—
about the same as this man makes
with his six-day weeks, twelve-hour days. He's not
quite sure about his age. 'Fifty,' he says,
'or forty-six.' Sixty, I would say.
I pinch a peanut off the plate, harmless
if I skin it. Then risk the tea, offend
by shoving back those squares of cake. She says
they're called *gulabjamans*; I say donut holes
soaked in syrup, fool word for a silly sweet.
To leave, we duck her clothesline strung with bras."

Purdah

In my rooftop study in India, sitting
by the ancient charpoy a yard high, with lacquered
legs and marble inlay—a bed fit for a king—
I'm surrounded by portraits of the Rajput rulers,
at least seven generations of them, each grim
in his turban, clutching his sword that rests upon a carpet.
But just one of these tilted pictures hung with wire
includes a woman. In all the dozen paintings, etchings,
old yellowed photographs, there is only one woman.
And she is presumably beautiful, though I cannot
be sure because she sits at her husband's side draped
in a veil like a beekeeper's gauze. It would be amusing
if it were not so sad, my not being able to see her,
my knowing her face is remembered by no one alive now.
She wants to look out, to gaze down into my room.
Her small hand touches that veil of purdah as if
to lift it aside. But the faces of men next to her
are stern, with fierce angry eyes. These men hold swords
and wear turbans of power, their hair coiled and held
for a strike. They will not let her come out
into this century. And her beauty if it was beauty
is lost forever as magnesium flares against tile,
blinding those men while I presume her eyes
were brown agate, her skin the bronze of those women
of roadsides, who cup their gold hands as I pass.

Sociology

In December I went to the village
with the study group. We tramped around,
saw men digging a well with buckets
and two tugging oxen. Two of the girls
were lowered, laughing, on baskets deep
into the earth, grasping ropes, swaying.
The scholars counted milk-bearing buffaloes
and new calves that left teats
of the mothers glazed and gleaming.
And the students duly noted work hours
of village women—four A.M. to ten P.M.—
and made a Hindi entry about hostility
toward Education—it took females from farms,
fouled up the marriage market. No one would take
a woman who could read or who refused
to tend buffaloes. We sat round on a blanket
waiting for lunch bubbling in kettles.
Just then a woman shuffled by, looking dazed
as in a dream. She held her yellow sari
against her face, drew it aside to look
our way, then approached, stood near me
so that I saw the warped thin bones of her legs
and her silver ankle bangles fallen
upon splayed-stick feet. I thought
she wanted money, but the Muslim lady doctor
who had been holding forth, joking,
excused herself and led the woman away
into the kind of vacant lot that's used
for executions, a courtyard fallen
into disgrace, its trees picked bare by goats.
The two stood in glaring sun, only their heads
above the chunk of wall. But I could tell
the woman bared her body, spoke as if confessing.
The doctor nodded gravely in her black hood
like a Capuchin's, quaint burnoose of purdah.
She gave advice, patted the woman

kindly on her shoulder. I thought of how,
a few minutes earlier, the other women, all Hindus,
had said the doctor was letting women down
by wearing this archaic veil of purdah. And she
had said she wore it as sunshade only, no need
to chide her. Yet they reproved her, said she helped
sustain a vicious social problem. Crestfallen,
that doctor wandered back, fat and tragic now,
dark Muslim whose face caught light though bowed
in a prayer she mumbled. She did not look back
as the peasant woman wrapped again that yellow sari,
then drifted like a wraith across the field.
"She's had them both removed," the doctor said,
and bit her lip. "Too late. It did not help."
The subject closed, she bent again over her meal,
scooped with a chapati cupped in hand. The talk
went on, of milk statistics, how many wells
were dug that year by hand, how the village had just
one TV, which all castes shared—TV had brought
them together. But I went on thinking of that woman
who had lost all that mattered in a village formed of clay,
all she had to offer men in moonlight, and her babes
who scamper hungry in the night.

Funeral Procession

The body's jounced
in a hemp net held high
by joggling friends
who sing and let
roses, marigolds
fall onto the heads
of watchful wayside
dogs—little hats
of red and orange
for them. A woman
doing laundry
stops to watch.
Next time the bell's
for her, or so
her great eyes say
while the dripping
shirt she holds
waits like a white chicken
whose neck she'll wring.
Drops of water fall
like tears, catch
light that breaks
through leaden clouds
moving swiftly on,
like those
calm Buddha sat upon.

Peacocks

In a corner of the park's a little hut
shoulder high, its door propped tin,
and half the human life's outdoors
where the group sits round. Busy hands
scrape bowls, next to their beds of hemp.
But soon they'll rise to work. The father
rides his rickshaw, roaming far. The mother,
granny, kids all clip and glean. No blade
of grass or herb or seed is wasted here,
nor would you find prodigious litter left
the way it is at home. All's used, to tie
another shoe at least, and jewelry's made from junk.
There's nothing worthless, not here
where these splendid iridescent chickens of the poor
pick through ash, flash blue sapphires, green emeralds,
keep guard with a thousand eyes. At night
they find a roof, watch for the great monsoon.

A Family

Underneath a sign's
the only home they have.
They've tied a rope
to make a swing. The oldest
hugs a swaying tire
above his brothers, who squat
in sand beside their mother,
who labors to make breakfast
although it's not quite clear
what way she plans to heat it.
The youngest tugs her breast
while yet another waits.
The father shines his rickshaw,
on which he hopes to earn
ten rupees, more or less
a dollar, if he works
past midnight, pushing pedals
for tourists from
the Rambagh and local ladies too
who sit behind him
like happy pigeons, silk
saris out in wind
as they fly past signs
and families in sand.

Elysium in the Halls of Hell

Tireless in his red turban
he plays his six-stringed *ramsha*
like a rickety violin.
He's got silver anklets,
and red betel on his teeth.
His barefoot stomp on grass is what
the ardent tourists come for.
They also like the crimson
bougainvillaea, snake charmer
with his burlap bag of cobras,
his tethered mongoose sniffing,
and those umbrella roofs
of terra cotta over
long verandahs with marble arches.
And there are costumed women
with bare bellies who pass
and repass the gate, seen through
the mist of fountains, a flash
of local color. Afternoons
the pool is fine for lounging
nearly, but not quite, nude.
Even birds upon the grass
are a part of paradise. Peacocks
are commonplace, like jewels
in shops along the corridors.
But I could take these tour groups through
that green western wall of leafy trees,
just across the road, in fact,
where a pig strolls from a shack,
where human mothers nurse in burrowed sand,
could lead them up that alleyway
and show them what they would rather fail
to see. It moans and sighs, and the human breath
of it at night can reach even
the hotel's latticed windows where once
the harem women strolled, peeked out.

The Progress of the Soul

I've grown quite good at ignoring them,
these street beggars who show their sores,
old women with gnarled hands, agony
on their faces, first-rate at visualizing
how they suffer or pretend to, making
the motions of eating, busy with hand
at mouth to show us—and pointing to
the baby held, his brown legs dangling
as if he's dead already, his belly swollen.
I've grown quite good at not seeing this,
wading right past on my way in-
to the restaurant or the shop, looking
their way only on occasion to consider
taking a picture. In the case
of the beautiful legless girl pulled around
on a child's wagon by her husband I simply acted
as if I had not seen her, but knew I had
to get a picture of her lovely oval face
gazing at me as if she were belle
of the ball, and all the while, her body
twisted, she sat on that child's wagon.
With the spider man, walking on his hands
and heels, I used a telescopic lens,
and yet he saw me, stopped and cupped
his hands, rushed toward me with a speed
I'd thought impossible. They catch us
as we descend from rickshaws or from porches
of the restaurants where we have fed well,
where I am always tempted to offend
my friends by bringing out leftover chapatis
or half-full bowls of soup. Yet I am quite good
at it, practically blind already, looking right
past them, even through them, avoiding
the cacophonous music of their coughs,
their lungs rattling like snakes so dangerously
near us, and it is tempting to give

some of the change, but we must plan
for tomorrow and I know that next time
they would claw me to shreds. As it is
they are grabbing my elbows, saying "Sahib, Sahib."
They are regular Sahib sisters. I believe
that soon they will notice how I am blind now,
no longer American, virgin, easily shocked.
Soon I will wade through the forest
of them rocking their little brown dolls
turned out in profusion and plenty as if
it's Christmas each day. Even the four- and five-
year-old girls act like mothers, have babies
to rock. They all wail to the skies,
a sulphurous lament I'll swear is worse,
far worse, than smog hugging our cities back home.

Address to a Child

Oh, child of Shivaji Park, do not fear
that I fail to notice your virtues—not the least
of which is lifting your sister. She's as big
as you are; you squeeze her too tight,
and she'll run if you let her. I assure you your smile's
already approved. You greet me each day here
not with voice but with eyes big as those agates
we thumbed as schoolboys on knees. You're Friday
to my Crusoe, follow me about, barefoot and worshipful—
filthy ragamuffin with rag mop of hair, mask
of teeth and eyes, little savage for sure. Strange
we love each other wordless as we do. And yes,
I admire your little fire made of sticks, green
ashoka leaves that give off an incense. No harm,
can't burn down a desert. And I see you count bugs,
just as my sister did, ladybugs, ants. When I leave,
I'll think of you often, I promise, like farm cousins
who stay to know poverty, pain, and disease. Yet I pray
you'll not lose that talent for lifting a stranger
as high as your gaze can, till he's light
as gift of your slow smile can make him. Namaste,
my child.

A Well in India

A gleaming pulley creaks. Two oxen tug.
The frayed rope quivers, lifts the bag
of a camel's skin again and again all day.
In fifty years you might return and find
the same wet camel skin, the oxen, man
like this man, brown-skinned farmer you
have seen in Bible illustrations, hand
at his oxen's yoke. He has been here ten
thousand years and his routine has been
designed to last forever, oasis in a sea
of chaos. He's unaffected by the world
beyond his center. Breeze off fields
is gentle, air not fouled, and the stick
he idly flicks upon his oxen's back
is no more than a twig. You spend an hour gazing
at him, who sees this same horizon all his years—
a few palm trees, a distant mountain every time
he turns. Ten thousand years like this
and he's found a way to plod in one tight circle
without remorse—by tugging at a rope that lifts
a camel skin, his oxen munching. He would not know
the word for boredom, just plods and does
that work. His function is the guiding of his ox.
And he himself wears harness lightly, a single leather rein
looped round his waist. The women come with jugs
upon their heads, approach the silver water splashing.
You'd like to stay, wordless, caught in sun, freed
of what's ordained for you, who share a bell note tinkling.

Villagers

They do nothing halfway here,
scatter, hide behind reeds
and corners of clay, peek
over dung walls—or all rush out
coaxing their nanny goats near,
showing their almond-eyed maidens
as if you must choose or take all.
(Veils drop from stunned faces.)
They drag up on charpoys in dust
their sick and their dying for your
blessing, for sure as hell
you're ordained by one or more gods.
The small boys beg you with smirks
to make them immortal in one fading
snapshot. Yellow and warped on a wall
it may yet bring good luck.
Right now they're not doing so well.
Water is twelve miles away;
women bring it in jugs
on their heads. The blacksmith
pursues his art by the roadside
as if there's a Bronze Age ahead.
All he needs is his fire, his boy,
and his tongs. Next time you'll bring
salve for his sores, a surgeon
to cut off a limb that offends.
At doorways the ladies wash hair
and pick one another's head lice
with the grace of houris of paradise.
If you pause and gaze toward them
they'll stand up and dance,
or so their amused eyes seem to promise.
If you ever come back they will rush
out to embrace you, long-lost exile
returned to the dust of your streets.

The Hundred-Year-Old Scotch in Rajasthan

When I drank the hundred-year-old Scotch
we were sitting at a long table on a terrace
and were much admired—the turbaned Rajputs and I—
by the villagers gazing over the waist-high walls.
We were well served and expansive, having eaten
our fill more than once and already paraded
through the mud streets to the joyous accompaniment
of everyone who could move, whether on crutches
or carried in arm. And the music was made by whatever
drum they could play or tin horn. Somehow
the noise managed its message medieval. I was proud, of course,
to be for once with the winners, the aristocrats.
It must have been clear to all that I was the honored
foreigner, and yet I was aware that it was not,
so to speak, personal. Any foreigner would do.
Simply being there made me a god. Well into evening
the bearers kept filling my cup, and when we moved on
to the castle for dinner—on a turreted roof, sitting
in great easy chairs as Arab sheiks do in movies—
the food was hot with spices, so I had to drink more
and more, there being no water save what was hauled
from the step-well, and I had already seen them
bathing there, stepping down to the square pool
and having a good splash, washing their hair as well
as their bodies, then drinking from cupped hands.
None of that stuff for me, not for a Westerner.
So I kept drinking the pleasant amber-colored Scotch,
and asking of one beaming host after another
if this was not indeed the hundred-year-old Scotch,
and was assured again and again I was in effect
drinking pure gold, liquified. Dawn found me
walking out under palms through the fields—for all
India as a toilet has been well and accurately said.
The man at my side, on a similar quest, a Rajput
aristocrat with great mustaches and bronze skin
said, "Sahib, we are so happy you are alive this morning;

we thought you would surely be dead." I had one hell
of a headache and I trembled, but the main thing
was that I needed a place in the fields to squat.
Others were already busy at it, spread out, each
with a little bucket set beside him, water for washing.
"What do you mean?" I asked. "That hundred-year-old Scotch
was terrific. But I drank more than I should." Headache
was not all that I throbbed from. And the man laughed
like a demon of sorts. He stopped in the sun rising,
gilding the fields, then he laughed wildly, almost
in hysterics. "Hundred-year-old Scotch, Sahib?
That was only our *first* drink. The rest was from here
in the village. They use the old car radiators
for distillers. Already this year six die in this village
alone. The lead in those car parts, it is poison."
"But why," I asked him, almost in tears, not sure now
I'd live to eat breakfast or until noon or even until
I managed to squat in the field, "why did that bearer
keep serving?" "Oh, Sahib," the Rajput explained,
"you liked it a lot. We Rajputs could see that,
and we remarked to each other how happy you were.
That bearer, he wished to be nice."
                                        "Nice?" I yelled.
"Knowing maybe I die from it?" "Oh yes," he said,
"for that is our custom. We must always be *nice*."
I was not well enough to continue our discourse,
so I staggered on till a few riverside rushes
gave me the chance to touch mother earth
and deposit half or more of my body, then some of my tears
while much of me died there, came to know
what the phrase meant, one hundred years of solitude—
which I then suffered within one square yard of Indian earth.
And yet I recall it gleaming like gold—the first glass
of that hundred-year-old Scotch in Rajasthan,
and how those eyes over the wall admired and envied me
for drinking it, holding the glass up for another, and another.

The Roadmenders

Through bankrupt countries where they mend the roads.
—W. H. Auden

Grandmothers mend the roads, lifting
their great pans high, heavy with sand
or gravel. They stoop in the dried-up
riverbed to dig the fill, squatting to chop
some stone as if it were a garden cabbage.
Young girls mend the roads here,
sun drying them up like vines, and their fruit
goes withered in fumes from lumbering buses
whose Punjabi drivers curse
to be caught in such lowlands
and hell, such potholes for wheels.
Such a ditch and these winding
trails should not even exist,
dug out by hands because the flood
has broken the heart of a bridge,
refuted its excellent logic,
fractured its place in the landscape.
For the gods want the roads
worked on, the supernumerary,
crooked, leprous, accursed roads,
want penance for the lives
of these women, the lives they spent
elsewhere, dancing, carousing with the mad emperor,
strolling in the green and cool gardens.
For such reasons, because of the gods
and their convictions against good bridges
and bad women, the formerly bad women
mend the roads, stooping in the sun,
lifting heavy mattocks and those pans
upon their heads. And if they complete
one road they can begin another—
the one stretching off into the distance,
twisting like a lazy serpent in the sun.
And at night, let them braid
the long black hair of their daughters.

The Armory

Two minutes and you've got the general
idea, though of course the guide can make it
more specific, how the tarnished weapon is sharp,
could slice your own slim neck. He has quite
a sense of humor, wants a rupee, tells
how the crossbow was deadly to horsemen
if fitted with the special point he holds.
Knives hide here inside knives inside more knives,
like little fish in open mouths of big.
And there are hidden bullet chambers in
half the handles of harmless-looking canes.
There's a rifle that in truth's a cannon
for blasting to hell the good Friar Bungay.
I say the place is rank. No goods unused
here. Walls hold great palm leaves, except they're spears.
Scimitars arranged make spread claws of crabs.
The scabbards are mostly velvet, the curved
blades thin as nails, practically translucent.
I get the point. Man does his best to kill.
Yet the quiet in this museum room
is quite incredible, would mock the men
who had their thumbs chopped off—or maybe heads—
when one of these blades beautifully fell.
Outside there's sunshine shimmering and air
perilous with scandal and appetite,
and a rickshaw to take you toward your death.

Little Incident

One day, quite lost,
riding my bicycle,
I turned into a gateway
where a sign in English
read NURSERY, and I rode
between rows of African violets
and banana trees in big pots.
The red-blossomed gold mohar
tree shaded my face, and bars of
neem-tree saplings fell past me.
And then I saw through leaves
the children laughing at me, sitting
in their circles or playing
in the sand, for this place
was indeed a nursery, the greenery
only incidental ornament
to shade their faces.
And then their mothers came
toward me with open arms
to swoop their children up,
a river of love and colorful saris
gold-fringed and blue, and I wished
I too were a small child with such
a mother coming toward me,
gleaming and ripe with sister inside her.

A Human Donkey

The boy who tugs that cart along
is ten perhaps, a human donkey
put out to work. His bare feet pad
on the hot tar of India.
Great sweat drops roll off his brow.
He's got a load of rolled canvas,
the kind we've seen staked to corral
a crowd eager to see a film
or used for walls of privacy
at weddings. This canvas is strong
as ship sail, with bright swastikas
appearing in every panel
for good omen. It's heavy too,
as that boy's effort shows. He leans
forward as if into the wind
and is nearly tipped off the ground
when he takes that awkward turn
that will take him away from me,
past an angled concrete delta
under giant billboard lovers
who can speak only in Hindi.
They almost kiss yet manage well to see
out over the crowd of rickshaws.
Smoke from the peanut stand obscures
him now. He disappears in haze,
a boy put out to labor, flagged
with his blue bandana, tugging
the flat-bed cart that's set upon
a truck's sheared-off axle, between
two tread-worn tires at least twenty
years older than this boy who's been
put out to work in India.

Grapes of Wrath

A nice little mess
they've made of it
here at the south edge
of Delhi, using three
bulldozers to rake
away the huts, tents,
jugs, and stacks
of bricks where they—
the untouchables,
or "former untouchables"—
built their fires,
cooked their meals.
One shack of cardboard,
burlap, tin had a woman
in it. They broke
her hip, that's all,
while the police
beat up those gathered round
who seemed not to like
this action. One man lay down
before the blades, grandson
of Gandhiji, or so
he claimed. Just one
man killed, head
broken with a club;
no one not wretched
need be at all concerned.
Yet two women, Gita
and Ramkali, even while
dozers shoved at their walls,
gave their babies
to light, now sit
and nurse them
in shade of rubble, scrub
of green, their faces determined and grim.

Near the Red Fort

This is Ghalib's city,
puddles and beggars,
no progress, only
more squalor. Yet here
he saw his bright slave girls,
desired them by daylight
and firelight, went madly
singing through streets,
drunk and ecstatic. Today,
deep into a year
cursed from the outset,
bus curtains sway.
The black hair on strangers
was stolen from harems.
Rickshaws are thick
as sticks in a flood,
cages for crickets. Rain
catches filth from the air,
consigns it to rivers in gutters.
My sadness has murdered
all the children of cheer,
bronze faces agleam
in black haloes of hair.
Their dark shadows taunt me,
begging for bread, begging for love.

The Bus from Delhi

In Delhi you wait for a bus in a courtyard
and over in a corner is a little shack
where they'll sell you Cokes, Limcas, water
you can trust if you're crazy. Bus pulls in late
and suitcases are strapped on top like a stagecoach.
You get the seat up front by the windshield
across from the driver who does not quite
look at you because you're a foreigner. Then you head out
twisting through streets, people parting to make way, not
too much mobbed today by their standards, yet it wouldn't take
much to set off a new riot. This is the scene
of some of the worst. You gaze over heads. A strange
stillness. Sacred cows wander. Auto-rickshaws galore
in bumblebee colors. More buses—the drivers waving
just as they did when you were a child. You gaze at all this
as if nothing's exotic, not the wildest of garbs spotted
from your excellent seat. You take all that's offered
for granted as if you'll be back, your regular route.
Losing the town, you settle in for the two hundred miles,
put your feet up where the wide window trembles. And you hope
the murdering dacoits aren't waiting ahead, making this day
another they'll write up in the papers, when blood
becomes just another jejune fact, not so exciting
once you get there. From the air you'd have seen nothing.

Peasant Girl

Any spot which a cow has condescended to honor with
the sacred deposit of her excrement is forever afterwards
consecrated ground, and the filthiest place plastered with
it is at once cleansed and freed from pollution. . . .
—*A. C. Bosquet*

What could I do this morning
after she smiled like that
—as open as any wife has been
on any wedding night—
but stop with some excuse
and so I took her picture
backing her off a bit, getting
in the frame the bare-bottomed
child she held but not
the other three who stood
beside her gawking.
Nor will the snapshot
show she's pregnant with yet
another. But it will catch
that smile as if she loves me
more than anyone who's strolled
for a longer time into my life.
And as we parted I gave
bananas to them all. The babe
just barely grasped hers
and looked confused, had ash
upon her belly. One small son
looked up at me with eyes
that wept, and then I moved
along, not knowing how
to follow to some hut stuck in sand.
And only then I noticed
that basket on her head—
of cow dung fresh and wet,
used for fire and rubbing on their walls,

and medicine and twenty other things.
And up on top of that steaming pile
was one fresh ball that gleamed
like a gold chignon,
as if the cow had laid
an egg on straw, without a crack.
She held that basket on her head,
one hand to steady it,
outlandish hat
worn just to humor me or take
to some grand fashion show.
She and the three who toddled by her side
took the sand dunes to my left.
Abandoned and bereft, I felt
her gaze upon my face
like sting of ivy dying.

In Bombay

On the way back to the hotel that night
a rat kept pace, turned the corner
when I turned beneath the palm,
then paused just when I did, though I meant
to let him go on, sniffing the wall.
He gazed expectant, waited, as if to offer
what those of two legs had, opium
and girls, "homosex," and black-market money,
disease no doubt, and naked dancers,
and a good jazz band, "here from Holland."
When I went on, he did too, waddling,
a hairy well-fed rat, taking the lead, quite
at home in his city of Bombay. He led me
as if he were my pet, sniffed toward
a family sleeping on the sidewalk,
his choice of what to show me.
The woman's arm sprawled across my path
as if she needed some injection.
She was lovely as a bride, her thin
gown red silk from an ancient harem.
Next to her, her husband was turned
against the wall, and a naked child lay
between them. The rat sniffed her cheek.
She sighed in sleep. I was impressed
by how these sleepers trusted us,
the rat and me and all the others
who would stroll by in the night.
Next day a poet told me there's a wall
across the beach, a kind of barricade
behind which those pavement-dwellers go
two by two to make their love—
conjugal love allowed like that
in well-run prisons—on the sand
in moonlight while the sea laps near
with mournful music eager to clean bones.

Mammalapuram

In Mammalapuram by the sea you saw
half-naked men dig in the shells
of peanuts tossed in mud.
They searched through each one,
already cleaned out, would lick
even a thin, papery red skin.
You saw that, my daughters, in India,
something I once saw in America
while dirigibles floated in blue skies
of the thirties, when we boys
burned Hitler in our trash barrels,
when alleys were crowded with hoboes—
men bending, stooping, searching.
And you saw a blind beggar
speaking Tamil, begging of another,
who turned up his face, pointing
to his own eyes, saying, "Friend,
I am one of you." Then another
led him toward us, foreigners
who would be his salvation,
and he showed us the gaping wounds
of his eyes. I took you halfway
round our globe for that,
not for the world's greatest
bas-relief, elephant in granite
slipping down mountains to the Ganges—
but for those beggars, so you might see them,
believe them, know how it was,
how it will be, our eyes burning like fire,
our wounds gaping and red and accusing.

At a Fortress in India

What I recall about Golconda,
that fortress on a hill,
is not the guidebook stuff or where
they picked the Hope diamond up,
but sharing out the peanuts,
hot and roasted, as we climbed,
littering the imperial stairway
where the fat king was carried
by his slaves, up and still farther
up, until he could look out upon
the Deccan tableland and brood
on his enemies, think, no doubt,
of what he had waiting for them,
boiling oil at the gateway
or melted lead, take your pick.
"They pour down oil
on your elephant," said the boy
who sold hot peanuts, told us where
to clap our hands to get heard far
above where the tunnels wound
like whorls of a conch shell.
And there were murder holes above us
for dropping giant stones on heads.
And if all else failed,
the fatal *vish kanya,* girl
of the harem, fed day by day
on poison until her kiss
was like a cobra's—she was sent
for special cases.
                              Of course we saw
the dungeon too, where a captured Hindu
scratched stone walls for years,
and the labyrinth for ladies. Both
caves had that square of light

that prisoners call the sky—I marveled
how they had hacked such holes
from solid rock, four feet. That sultan
was so gross I wondered
who helped him with his harem,
placing women round him
like pillows or tender melons.
I think the urine reeked
even then in weeds, when he defended
his fortress and the great Siva lingam
hacked out near the top and left erect
by Hindus whom he had conquered.
He lost his war at last
to that beast Aurangzeb,
who relied on treachery, since all
the snares of rock worked well.
Up high atop the fortress we note
the view all round,
our hair strung out in wind. Across
the plain I spot
a lake adorned with white egrets. We eat
more peanuts, also spot
that monumental Charminar, in the old
town center, put up
because they beat the plague
in 1591, though the plague returned—
that's why it's called the plague.
And you are right, my hostess, we should
indeed come back quite often and together,
climb this fort, circumambulate
the outer walls, which look much like
the Great Wall of China.
But we won't. I linger longest
in the ruin of the harem,

where countless little shelves
like Gothic doors held candles
which lit their dancing. I prowl
their pool, no water there,
but swings still hang in air, anchored deep
in rock, rust the color of their flesh,
pegs of iron for where
they splashed and played. I notice
that grass like hair
blows gently in the breeze, cracked stone.

Light failing strikes a pool, pure scum,
while we come down past piles
of cannon balls and stacked gun barrels.
We crane our necks toward murder holes again,
again emerge unscathed, are chauffeured back
through dusty streets in frenzy, alive
with the Diwali holiday, carts and shops
full of orange and yellow marigolds, all meant
to drape our necks, also sweets and fireworks
(one called the Atomic Bomb), and dolls
that are gods, to worship from our honking car.
Rattling rickshaws scatter. Noise is like the Fourth
or firing on Fort McHenry. The holiday
means this: their great god Ram returned from distant
travels, having cut off all ten heads
of the monster Ravan; they light night skies
with fireworks because another monster (whom Ram
had packed off to the Underworld)
once promised to return and destroy everyone
on this darkest night of the year. Wisely they keep
the sky lit up with their wild infernal noise,
spend millions on rockets to scare
this beast away. Who wants darkness,

we well might ask, if it means the end of all
life on earth? And it makes more sense, I think,
than the arms race round the world. Planes weave
among the Roman candles bursting
like flak from World War II. From hovels round
for miles come flashes in the sky
like lightning, till you're sure
they're blowing up themselves.

                                      Later I recall
that breathless maid you brought along,
middle-aged and vacant-eyed
like one long lost, who had watched
her only son, age four,
brought down by a rabid dog, mad teeth bared,
slick with slaver, out of nowhere leaping
as if sent from hell for that. On Golconda's stairs
she pinched the cheek of a beggar boy,
pinched him hard and loving
like a piece of fruit. I thought she'd weep,
or steal that child. At the sultan's tomb she fell
upon her knees the way she scrubs your floors,
prayed a Buddhist mantra. She's Hindu *but*
better safe than sorry, wore a bright
marigold in her hair, black wires
streaked with grey. And she loved me, I could see,
because I gave her peanuts and asked her
what her name was: Neela, meaning blue.
When I left your home, she waved through
the iron bars of her shadowed room.
She was pregnant from some gardener
to replace the boy she wept for. They say
her karma's bad, twice-robbed
since the poor boy died. And his picture
taken too—senseless, brutal wounds

in her heart beneath her sari. She reminded me
of my mother, her hat in cinders
from fireworks on the Fourth, a thousand griefs
to weep for. "This is what," you said,
"living in India is really like,
snared in your servants' lives. They'll break
your heart." And I replied, "Only if you let 'em."
At least cold stones will not do that. We climbed
them at Golconda, a smile on each
of our half-perceiving faces.

The Ganges at Dawn

A black crow finds his chunk of skull,
eats it on a rocking boat. Girls
with clinging saris duck their heads,
shampoo, cup drinks before they rise,
give way to others. Two small dogs
lie within a bed of ashes, last night's
cremation embers still aglow around them.
They're curled so blissfully, pretzel-
boned, like netsuke, porcelain,
you'd think they'd been fired into life
upon those kilns whose flames shot high:
thus souls of men rushed into dogs
despite the ancient promise—all
who by the Ganges die or burn
go straight to Hindu heaven. We stood
and watched those fires last night,
first one corpse, then another burned
while our rickshaw wallah cautioned,
"No good to think at night, just day."
But still we gazed, and watched the Doams,
men of that caste who touch the dead.
With a burlap pad one threw a foot
back in the flames. Pale pelvic bones
of women held out best, as if
the work of love and birth drew forth
from earth some stony strength, hard wood
at least. It sputters in those hips, boils
till they break apart like sticks of neem.
Hearts burn quickly, if not Shelley's.
And now at dawn, while thousands bathe
and the bridge fades in a sudden fog,
we watch young pups nose through grey ash.
They love that warmth, that bony hearth.
And yogis squat upon their ghats.

Some on all fours, it seems, make love
to splendid women made of air.
They mumble prayers. We're off today
for Khajuraho, where temples rise
to Tantric love. Stone couples there
for a thousand years tremble yet
at their passion's brink. Two girls lift
a third upon a man most triply blessed.
And all, the scholars say, to show
how we should kill the fiend Desire,
eschew most apples of our eyes.
First we leave the holy river,
buy eight flutes from a Hindu boy
who bargains poorly, drugged by fumes
and Ganges mist, forbidding greed.
We step past bodies, mummies wrapped to wait
their turn, join air and swirl as smoke.
Small babies, though, are gifted to the waters,
tied to a stone and bundled. A priest squats
in a boat, lets go this soul into the lapping waves.
The mother bravely stands to watch.
There's no farewell my words can say.

The Rickshaw Wallah Told Us

we should see the Taj in moonlight,
and full moon was out that night.
Thousands jammed the streets. We knew
they scanned long pools
to catch that moon and love's
monument, orgasm captured once
and for all time in white stone (except
for refinery air, not visible at night).
And many trudged, no doubt, into
that tomb—of love remembered well—
to see by candle flame
where Mumtaz, queen much adored,
still lay beneath
her inlaid stone, carnation-red
carnelian, green stems of emeralds.
But we stayed behind in that cheap hotel
and later swore we saw it, Taj
in moonlit splendor.

Agra Near the Taj

We were in Agra near the Taj when I went native,
bought thin pajamas, white and cool. And what a breeze
then struck! I was almost naked, and accepted
by the locals. They said to throw away my hat,
then entirely pass. But there was still
my Jack Armstrong all-American walk. I had moved
a step away, though, as the tourists clearly showed me.
They mocked in such a not so subtle way I got to know
just how it felt to be a wog. And when my wife and daughter
got quite good at kathak dancing, it was quite a shock
to those who came to see the culture to watch white
faces, bellies, naked toes with silver rings on. "I recalled
with happy face the shampoo you gave me with your feet,"
an ancient lyric ran. Made no sense until I saw that dance.
And at the five-star Clark Hotel, they had put the Russians up,
"engineers," they said—much like the CIA. By the pool
with bodies fat like babies they sucked their secret mission
out of mint-julep glasses. Upstairs their wives had hung
huge brassieres from windows. And their perfect children,
Ivans and Angelicas, slammed into the turquoise water.
Local rumor had it their mission was to clean the Taj
and whiten up the dome. But a counter-rumor claimed
they only meant to smudge it. Breeze through my legs,
cool as Gandhi's diaper, I strolled the dusty streets
past ladies stacking pots on heads, a Guinness record daily.
Thousands rode their bikes right at me. Traffic
was sheer terror. Peacocks seemed to know me now. My exile
seemed a fact, one more damn fool thing I'd done.
Yet all folks wished me well, for a stamp or a single coin
long lost in a forgotten pocket,
the one that had held my watch before time stopped.

The Tour Group

At the crowded Ganges once I hitched a ride
with tour-group tourists in their bus.
They had let me join them for that trip
to the airport through seven miles of city,
more of countryside. The members of that group
wore wide-brimmed straws, sipped Cokes, showed
    trinkets
they had bargained for, flutes,
jade, bronze, saris, bamboo back scratchers—
sandalwood and camphor—carved figures they had
no idea were gods. At dawn they had checked out
of the five-star hotel with the fine swimming pool
to see the Ganges River, all
that pageantry of craziness, monks
in prayer, girls bathing, cremation fires.
And all along they obeyed injunctions
not to touch or taste. And then through glass
as honking horns parted the human sea
I saw the world as they had seen it always.
Out in the fields the peasants looked
like tableaux in museums. On lovely heads
that bobbed along, the women lifted firewood.
Men plowed dry earth with nothing much but sticks
while bare, redundant boys ran everywhere.
Below our tinted windows on a busy
roadside trail, a horde was fleeing war,
their life possessions on their heads.
Their bodies gleamed from what was surely heat.
And yet I had to guess, for in that air-conditioned bus
I felt no sense of life out there. The scene
outside might well have been a movie. That's how
we see the world now, from air-conditioned rooms,
from bombers ten miles high. Yet now and then
above that music, humming tires, or through
the aery contrails streaming, entrails
across the poisoned sky, a voice gets through:

our leader singing of his loves: the merchant kings,
the royal, the "rich and famous," justly idle,
who adorn the latest gilded age.
And he tells us of his hates: the welfare
cheats, cripples, hungry kids—blight
upon our landscape. And he smiles to think
on beauty bare: those shiny missiles, rockets,
vats of poison gas, pits of peril, glowing pools
of woe, debt to bind the ages. I heard him,
in those twangy tones from home, that tour-group
horde, and thought of Gandhi too, whose voice
rose up through heat and dust: "I saw the tears
of the oppressed." Two voices, contrapuntal.

Yama

The horror is that there is no horror.—*A. I. Kuprin*

One night in India with our daughters
we stayed in a cheap hotel, taking the two
front rooms, and all night coming and going
in the dim-lit hall were men who had something
to say to the giggling women in mostly red
who stood outside doors farther back.
There was a bar with a jukebox and a heavy smell
of burning joss and perfume, and I went out,
crossing the hall many times during the night
to sit over a beer and contemplate this immense
action and listening to the murmur in Malayalam
and now and then in Hindi, like currents
that wove round one another, sensual, friendly,
amused. And yet I myself did nothing,
as I always do nothing. I gawk and pretend
I do not know what is happening. That's the only
trick I know—devised originally somehow
to survive, when I was a boy in the dark. I did not
know that man was beating the woman. I did not know
that child was being destroyed by the prurient
paws of the old fool. But years later in India
I was alert all night—and, somehow charmed
by my own gratitude, the warm glow, we might say,
as I thought of my family, those girls
who slept innocent and ignorant in the front room
with open mouths and no more peril than a few
　　mosquitoes.

Ajanta

When we went to the caves at Ajanta, the bus
at last stopped at a lookout and we tourists
gazed past an iron rail at a grand horseshoe bend
in the river. The temples far below had been hacked out
of cliffs, inset in rock, columns at cave mouths
propping the mountain. We gazed through the air
at this sight still a half mile away. An old man coughed,
threw his cigar out toward a crow afloat far below us.
Boys nudged our elbows, asked if we would buy souvenirs
—before we were there—a geode perhaps, plucked out
of moonscape and cracked to reveal a jewel jagged and blue,
and possibly radioactive, for each seemed to glow.
We had more miles to go—twenty-three kilometers winding
down to the caves in that rickety bus. There we found
souvenir stalls; their *objets d'art*, mostly from Hong Kong,
had little to do with the caves or with Buddha, e.g., a Russian
doll turned out on a lathe. One opened up to give birth
to another inside her until there were four, just like us.
We crawled in and out of those caves, touched one Buddha
    reclining
as if for a nap. He was twenty-three feet from hair knot
to toe. He was huge and I rubbed his smooth belly. The Japanese
were offending him with flash bulbs, then tossing the spent cubes
aside on the cave floor as if that's how they offered their gifts
to the gods. All the statues were impressive, though hidden
in shadows for years, overlooked till an Englishman chasing
a tiger nearly fell off a ledge of the plain down to the river,
past the great caves. I wondered if monks had found peace there,
sitting in cells, chanting their mantras, knowing no more
of the world than that view out through the cave's mouth,
through columns like giant bars of a prison, out to a space
over the river that had carved cliff face of that horseshoe
as if with the power of mind. When we came out in the late
afternoon I observed up high, where we had stopped, a plowman
turning his oxen away from the space that went blue in haze,
where fields left off, where mind might be said to begin.

The Caves

The ancient texts will give you plenty of reasons
there is no God or if there were how he would not
be half inclined to think of you, or to have made
the world and you in the first place. He'd have
no interest at all in Matter, having none of his own
to slow him on his perpetual ethereal travels.
Come to think of it, he wouldn't bother to travel.
Those wits who sat in caves among carvings had time
on their hands, so they went on to argue the opposite—
how each effect naturally is caused by something
we have to call God or Krishna or Brahma or Rama
simply because he seems to have thought of everything,
then some more—like earthquakes, floods, and the savage
disasters man makes up as if by himself. Moreover,
God maybe gave monsters and devils and Ravana, the ten-
headed warrior. These assiduous monks before they were done
filled their caves knee-high with pure logic. And sculptors
carved the walls round, their dust drifting on manuscripts.
They created stone women and angels, believable visions
of lovers. A man can still, in fact, fall hard for a woman
in stone, archaic and chipped, with a body a million times
kissed. Today the silence hums over the hazed canyon. Sacred
river still cuts deep into bedrock beneath wading lepers.
And above the mouth of each cave, where a monk spun
out reasons and doubts, black bees swarm at their work now,
making honey that drops from wax cells. These bees could trace
their births back to Ashoka, that great Buddhist king
who left road signs for reaching Nirvana, state of bliss
like a city of swans and souls without purpose, with eight
noble paths and no more. A ninth would break a saint with a
feather, he who had taken a decade to learn each
of the four noble truths, he who had nearly missed the path
altogether, but found it in the dead end of a silent dark cave.

Heroes

Even the idea is absurd—heroes—in this day and age
when we have all been revealed to be lowly, worse
than dogs. But there we were, out in India, with Don
and Max trying to impress us with their round-the-world
balloon. And though marooned in the desert scrub of Rajasthan,
a land they'd never have chosen, they were living more or less
like Fitzgerald characters, cocktails and barbecues
by the pool of the five-star hotel, telling adventures,
holding forth. I loved it, and had on my best tweeds
to meet the ambassador, who had flown down from New Delhi
to greet these Americans. That's when it occurred to me,
there by the pool, that we were all heroic and adventurous.
Don and Max were telling how they had rocked over Iran,
guns of the Ayatollah about to be fired—they heard babble
of jet pilots swarming around, eager to blast them—
yet this was a tale calm and cool in the telling
while bearers and peons brought drinks, trays
of great melons sliced. In the background, the kohl-eyed dancers
paid devotions to Krishna, their palms pressed together
weaving the sky. And I asked one of the money-voiced wives
how she liked India, riding in rickshaws. "What's
a rickshaw?" she said, and I saw that her make-up
was heavy, slick silver reflective and powdery. Her blue
painted eyes might have been out of *Vogue,* and of course
she had not flown over in a balloon. "No siree!" she declared,
Pan Am for her—she laughed as if a close call had just
been averted. Afternoons at the edge of the airport
while peasants gawked, Don and Max posed for the press,
climbing in and out of their gondola, little spaceship—
something out of Jules Verne, its tackle collapsed
on the folded balloon. The two heroes crawled within,
waved through portholes as they would in the sky,
then beckoned in daughters and wives, glamorous, beautiful,

hugging and clowning. As, a few days later, Don and Max
crawled in for their flight—time after time delayed, awaiting
reports on the winds—I noticed their shoes, soft kid leather
like those worn by old men and bankers—a pathetic touch
  somehow—
and silk socks held up with garters beneath cuffs of astronaut
coveralls with insignia flags sewn everywhere. At last,
weather bright, they took off and were lifted to heaven—
brief ascension, for they crashed against a dung-walled village
crowding the mountains, the grand Himalayas. Once more
they were patched up and airborne, months later were killed
as they raced across Europe, tempting the gods again and again,
for that's what heroes have done always. I mourned not just
Don and Max, my friends out in India—heroes if any exist—
but the Idea itself, the Heroic. As I tried to make clear
that night by the pool, we should always hold out to the end,
follow our stars though they wobble and wink and betray us.

At the Hill Station

Not rickshaws here on the mountain, but carts
tugged by men. Or if you wish, you can ride
in a tea box a coolie lifts with a halter. I've seen
a few men, and many a woman—each bobbing inside such
a box—piggyback. But we said no to our girls,
spoiled enough as it was. Umbrellas are torn
by wind. Still, business is brisk. Many tourists head
for the top; there they can look out from
a roofed tea shop on stilts, see valley after valley.
There we've drunk our tea often, watched
another year pass, daughter becoming her mother.
I've neglected again that chore of all travelers,
did not bring my Nikon. So I miss that playful
black-eyed monkey pretending to weep,
rubbing knuckles on eyes. I sit down beside her
on the bench, watch clouds scud up the mountain,
blue haze fill the distance. A coolie trudges by,
patches on his pants, harness of ropes slung around him,
band crossing his forehead—enough weight for a mule.
His is an articulate trek, as his bones slide within
gleaming skin, straining his lungs, making his nose drip.
I hear him wheeze as he glances with a half grin sideways,
though he's bent from the weight of that fat lady
who looks pleased, jouncing around. He'll soon be
on cremation fire, or, if Parsee, will be placed
for the vultures high on a Tower of Silence.
Yet his eyes scan the slopes, eager for work on the way down.
Here come more monkeys, a troupe begging for baksheesh,
hands cupped like a human's, their eyes pleading. The mother
monkey's in a tattered dress, feeds her child all
scraps thrown by those amused tourists, most
up from the plain, their vacation at a hill station
the year's luxury—a trip to the tea shop, a purchase
of shawls. "Nay, nay." I shoo those monkeys,
refuse to pay for their tricks. I'm alone
as a saint in this town Kipling put in a poem.

The Lovers

We move to the hill station, for our friends are kind
enough to know that a foreigner cannot bear the hell
of heat and dust that's routine to them. We clear the air,
find mountain paths to stroll, and each day see tombs
that could well be in Sussex or some Yorkshire churchyard.
One yellow temple complete with pediment looks good enough
to live in, with terraced slopes below and winding path,
red blossoms like birds' nests in trees, Himalayas behind.
Moss grows thick enough to trickle over slopes, rain green.
Bronze plaque tells names. Neighbors have obelisks or angels.
Great pines lean, sough music in wind. I can almost see
this couple as they rounded the bend, a hundred years past.
He was a soldier, wounded while fighting Bengalis,
and she was the English nurse who loved him. Her eyes
were great brown orbs like yours, and her touch tender.
She stopped each morning beside that path to pluck
a red hibiscus for her hair. Then they continued on
around the curve we walk today, he with his cane like mine
but needing it more, she with her hand at his elbow.
A hundred years ago their love was gossip of this hill station,
hospital wards of the Raj. They felt no need to pick out
their tomb, little temple. Sharp perfumed air and blue iris
loud as glorious ghazal tell me they were here.
He could look in her eyes and see England.

Leaving

Thoughts of leaving jar me plenty.
Full circle upsets always—back to where
we started; again the plane with gleaming wings
awaits us, and like us all it's more fatigued now. Such
circles start at dawn, and so they end.
As with executions we endure the final night, assess
all it has been, this year, this life. I think
of Ved, who stood on a traffic island, waves
of rickshaws and sacred cows strolling round.
"For you," he said, "it is a one-year sentence,
for me it is life." What he perceived so clearly,
with sadness in his eyes, was fact indeed: I
would rescue no one. Like all who came and left,
I had not much to give. All journeys reaffirm this.
Before night pales they all arrive to hug us—
more friends than we left back home. They sit alert
as if for birth or death—and this seems both.
So we take a cab with bags tied on. Our daughters have
their final fling on scooters. They flutter
like bright flags, right up to the airport's door.
Then these bronze swains must leave them, and yet
quick vows might be exchanged. I turn from that.
With unenlightened eye I gaze on the waiting room.
We elders once more swap hugs, farewells, enact
that farce *we'll meet again*. As in some dream
we're pushed through rails and sorted out,
some to fly and some to stand their ground.
And who's to say who's lucky? To go's a death,
to stay a hell. Our final dawn together.
Just so, in Calabria, my friend Frederigo wept.
He would never see my small son Sam again,
held up in arms for farewell kiss, great tears
as our train pulled out. A man may weep, aye,

even a fat man weeps. And so we leave
our nests of straw, thorns through the chanting land,
leave old men inside smoke, leave florid crane
on one leg standing, stuck in primeval mud,
leave lady next to Buddha, and Buddha on his cloud—
while children on the ground behind us still stroke
hurt wing of a fallen dove. "To cure him"
is what they told me and wished me health as well.
A year with no man's curse, or child's,
and yet I did not stay. I did not stay and heal.

Back Home

A friend tells me of soup kitchens
and his work with the dying, those
whose eyes are bulbous with fear
of the here and beyond. "It's not all
in India," he says, and I agree (though
thinking of Calcutta), and I give
him ten bucks to help maintain
a hospice where all are kept well off
the floor, in crank beds angled
like ski runs—with lots to read, ice
cream on demand, flowers in light
and abundance—all higher than the stone
and dirt floors Calcutta nuns stoop to.
But there's never a hug in this hospice
run out of two zoned neighborhoods!
For that it would take Mother Teresa
or some other saint, lifting a burden
in such a way that Love could be said
to triumph, while Death is not denied
the ecstasy it longs for.

Lobster

Gandhi, I know, would never approve. But urged
by my friends I assent, knowing "live lobster"
means dead, his reprieve cut short by my choice.
But of course "there's no pain." I say a few
words, stare at him as he's hauled once again up
where we can reach him, ruddled and crimsoned like sunset
far out at sea. He's been stalking the sand floor,
chunk out of ocean translucent, lit by fluorescence.
In the glass box he waves claws, idly searching
to pinch a philosopher's pebble we might drop
from above where we lean—or perhaps his bead eye
can see that innocent child in her fur, looking down,
seeking him. She picks out a toy she can eat.
And I too deliver my verdict, then turn on my heel,
wash hands as if it's been done, decreed by the gods—
like the killing Krishna demanded of Arjuna.
He is brought me, humbled, collapsed sculpture
of armor. I crack him with pliers, rinse his flesh
down with beer from a flagon, discard in fragments
that armor we crave but which he's grown, thick as steel—
yet no protection. The waitress sniffs our desires,
would love to serve tyrants. She removes a ruin
of shell, shrapnel—such scrap as litters the sea floor,
millions of years toward perfection. But overhead when we leave
he will rise resurrected, scoop in stars we can't even see.

Rickshaw Wallahs

You will long for their friendship—W. H. Auden

Back home for years now, we discuss the two rickshaw wallahs
who loved our two girls done up in their scarves, straw hats
they had to hold onto—men who pumped those bikes everywhere,
wobbling on greaseless wheels that creaked and groaned
while the customers sat and bounced *sans* springs, *sans* shock-
absorbers, *sans* much of a cushion. And yet it was better
than tongas, carts that joggled along like Grampa's wagon
back on the farm. How could these men love strangers so much,
the girls still want to know, care for them and write again
and again when they've had no encouragement? Surely it's not
just hope we will send them a dime sometime. These men
who sleep in alleys were as devoted as they come—ran up
to greet us by name months later, on our second trip to Agra.
And if we returned, though long lost now, they would still be
    loyal,
yet we think of them rarely and if we should pray for them,
including them in our circle, we'd judge ourselves naïve—
simple fools as they are to care so much, to love so uselessly.
Statistics say they're dead by now.

A Gas Cylinder

Two bucks will buy a cylinder of gas,
found now and then at yard sales slapped
with silver paint or orange, good as new
even if scratched up from ten years
of camping trips. You see them riding on
a trailer's tongue, underneath the plastic
window on an Airstream, or stuck in a truck-
bed. They're cheap, with a knob and nipple
to let gas flow. A rubber hose connects
the tank to a cooking range, iron grill or tin.
In India they will kill for one. You doubt
my word? But Delhi burglars kill indeed,
and often for this item, more precious than
a TV set, for instance. Near Jaipur when a flood
washed out a sudden chasm and the warehouse
collapsed and those small steel drums stored there
bobbed in the roiling waters, men waded out,
swam, poked sticks and poles and branches
to reach those toppling buoys. Some stood on shore
and offered bids, egged struggles on, and some
ventured too far, were engulfed. Several drowned,
seeking nothing more than a steel gas cylinder
or, in that frenzy, two or three to sell.
For such a trifling cylinder of gas, you say.
But if you do not have one there, your wife
cooks with kerosene that may well explode
and that makes her cough, die young—or for
a wood fire walks miles, strips what trees
are left, shared with goats. The man who longs
for a Honda scooter to pile his wife and kids on
finds status with this cylinder of gas
which the government makes him queue for—
don't ask me why; to ration the gas itself,
or simply to control, for the sake of control,

to keep those folks in line—and a long line
it is, stretching for miles, with thousands of names.
Or it's something else to bribe for, to be withheld
year on year. The worst fight that I had
in India was this—to get one—to enjoy
luxury the foreigner would find unthinkable
to miss. A bribe jumps queues. And when
you leave they fight for all you leave, no fight
more bitter than that fought round an orange
half-empty cylinder of gas left by a foreigner.
Back in the U.S. now, I gaze at such a one
in a yard sale line-up and the price comes down
to just a dollar. So I compute
the cost of shipment, then kick the hollow thing
to hear its tune, mere thud of air
more emptiness than not, like poverty itself.

Three Prayers: After Tagore

1. At midnight a bud opens in the dark forest.
   Even so I was not aware of that moment
   when I first came through
   into this life. Yet I knew where I was.
   And that force that made the bud open
   into the forest familiar and generous enough
   gave me into the arms of my mother.
   The bud knew all that was needed, and I too
   felt that same force without name.
   Death too is unknown,
   and yet then as well
   all will be given. The child cries out
   when removed from one breast but soon
   finds solace enough in the other,
   no less familiar, no less generous.

2. We know what we want, a route
   through the sky, through tangle
   of flowers, through stars scattered
   like stones. And it's denied.
   Route is obscured in all seasons.
   Yet they know where they're going,
   each flower opening on time, in its turn.
   After millions of years they are raised
   to their power, placed
   on their thrones, given their days
   in the sun, even among ruins holding on.
   And they never grow dark, sullen, hateful.
   That's why I pray to be like them.

3. When desire blinds the mind
                with delusion and dust,
   when my heart is hard as the others,
   that's when I need some of the mercy.
   It could not change *them*—no,
   but it might save me. I do not
   like it, this hardness of heart,
   this stone that I carry
   when there is no grace, when life
   is a sentence in the worst prison.
   And that's when I need
   some of the mercy, when I sit
   in the shadows, inside the shut doors.
   That's when I need some of the mercy,
   for that door to break open, giving out light,
   flinging away my monstrous despair.
   When desire blinds the mind
                with delusion and dust,
   O come, wakeful one, come
                with full light and thunder.

   Adapted from Rabindranath Tagore

The Razor's Edge

We found a cottage halfway up the mountain
and at the back was a small balcony with a table.
First thing in the morning, sometimes before dawn,
I would sit on that table cross-legged
like a Buddha and gaze off into the distance
over the vast valley below. There was no way
I could comprehend the pain there or the joy
in those swirls of dust that meant a town
far, far below on the great Ganges flood plain.
I could see the silver river twisting
like the amazing snake it's been called
so many times and in so many centuries.
But then those afflictions would float gradually up
and become a part of me so that I knew
my suffering was in those people too.
Then I would go in where giant spiders
on the wall were treated as friends,
where cobwebs could hang unmolested, where light
bumped from cloud to snow-topped peak and back
down to us, where my fiftieth birthday arrived,
a day I had never hoped to see. And I decided,
on a walk with you, under trees where great red
hibiscus flowers fanned out on both high and low
branches, that at last my life would be spent
as I would wish it. What little was left
I would live as wisely as I could, would take
each day as the blessing it was, nothing less.
And now already so much of that time
is missing in action, battlefield
like the other years, nothing but sculpture
in air created by gazing out from our lives.
Buddha himself might have managed it, Buddha
who did not seek, crave, tilt at windmills,
beg, claw toward the breast, apply, cringe,
approve or reject—Buddha who is still sitting
where I left him, looking out from the edge.

About the Author

The Maharani's New Wall and Other Poems is David Ray's response to a year in India. Awarded an Indo-U.S. Fellowship for 1981–1982, Ray lived with his family in Jaipur, where he was a visiting professor at the University of Rajasthan. He gave poetry readings throughout the country, and for a month he was a research scholar at the American Studies Research Centre in Hyderabad. He has written short stories about India and has published books in India that translate the Prākrit dialect into modern English.

Ray received his B.A. and M.A. degrees from the University of Chicago, and in 1966, after teaching at Cornell University and Reed College, he won a five-year Abraham Woursell Fellowship from the University of Vienna. In 1987, he served as exchange professor at the University of Otago, New Zealand. He was the founding editor of *New Letters* magazine and the creator of a weekly program for poetry over National Public Radio stations. Since 1971 he has been a professor at the University of Missouri–Kansas City.

Ray has won the William Carlos Williams Award of the Poetry Society of America, for *The Tramp's Cup,* a National Endowment for the Arts Fellowship for his fiction, and several PEN/NEA Syndicated Fiction Awards for his short stories. He is the author of many books of poetry, including *Gathering Firewood: New Poems and Selected* (Wesleyan 1974) and *Sam's Book* (Wesleyan 1987).

About the Book

The Maharani's New Wall was composed on a Mergenthaler Linotron 202 in Sabon, a contemporary typeface designed by the Swiss typographer, teacher, scholar, book designer, and type designer Jan Tschichold.

The book was composed by Brevis Press, Bethany, Connecticut, and designed by Kachergis Book Design, Pittsboro, North Carolina.

WESLEYAN UNIVERSITY PRESS, 1989